Alexander the Great

by

W.B. Godbey

First Fruits Press
Wilmore,
Kentucky
c2018

Alexander the Great. By W.B. Godbey.

First Fruits Press, © 2018

ISBN: 9781621717638 (print), 9781621717645 (digital), 9781621717652 (kindle)

Digital version at http://place.asburyseminary.edu/firstfruitsheritagematerial/...

First Fruits Press
B.L. Fisher Library
Asbury Theological Seminary
204 N. Lexington Ave.
Wilmore, KY 40390
http://place.asburyseminary.edu/firstfruits

Godbey, W. B. (William Baxter), 1833-1920.
   Alexander the Great / by W.B. Godbey. – Wilmore, KY : First Fruits Press, ©2018.
      34 pages ; cm.
      Reprint. Previously published: Cincinnati, Ohio : God's Revivalist Office, [190-?]
      ISBN: 9781621717638 (pbk.)
      1. Alexander, the Great, 356-323 B.C. 2. Providence and government of God. I. Title.

      BT135.G62 2018

Cover design by Jon Ramsey

asburyseminary.edu
800.2ASBURY
204 North Lexington Avenue
Wilmore, Kentucky 40390

First Fruits
THE ACADEMIC OPEN PRESS OF ASBURY SEMINARY

First Fruits Press
The Academic Open Press of Asbury Theological Seminary
204 N. Lexington Ave., Wilmore, KY 40390
859-858-2236
first.fruits@asburyseminary.edu
asbury.to/firstfruits

Alexander the Great

BY

Rev. W. B. Godbey

PRICE 10 CENTS

GOD'S REVIVALIST OFFICE.
1810 Young St.
CINCINNATI, OHIO

Alexander the Great.

"All things work together for good to them that love God" (Rom. 8:28) is a wonderful encouragement to every soul, giving us the victory on every battlefield, as we know, let it go as it may, it will prove a blessing to us if we are saved by the grace of God, and filled with His love. There is nothing so abundant and free in all the world as the grace and love of God.

The atmosphere envelopes the globe, resting on every inch of the earth's surface and mounting up thirty to forty miles high; and it is perfectly free for every air-breather, so that none need die for the want of air, if he will only keep his bodily organs open to receive it in its superabounding sufficiency for all.

Just so every person that has ever lived on the earth and even the devil himself, does God make a blessing to His true people. The awful battles we fight with Satan God doth surely make to us signal blessings, as the strong intellect of the devil, accompanied by his wonderful chicanery, ranks among God's grandest means of grace in the development of the nine graces—divine love, jo, peace, longsuffering, kindness, goodness, faith, meekness and holiness—by which we are saved and sanctified, and the nine gifts—wisdom, knowledge, faith, bodily healing, the working of dynamites, prophecy, discernment of spirits, tongues, and the interpretation of tongues—which constitute our panoply, with which we save others. By the nine graces we secure our personal salvation, the Holy Spirit imparting them in regeneration and perfecting them in sanctification, thus preparing us for a glorious immortality. Meanwhile those wonderful nine gifts so invest us with the whole armor of God as to make us omnipotently efficient in the salvation of others.

The reason why the athlete becomes the world's champion is because he fights with other champions. If his battles were all with pigmies, babies and dead people, he never would receive the muscular development such as made John Sullivan the champion of the globe. As the devil is the strongest foe, to God's true people he is the greatest source of blessing, because we all gain strength by the battle and courage by the victories we win over him and all his emissaries, excarnate and incarnate.

God uses unsaved people to do many things in the promotion of His kingdom in the earth. You may think it strange that people who lose their own souls and make their bed in Hell can be instrumental in saving and blessing others.

When I was Presiding Elder, thirty or forty years ago, the greatest revivalist in the district was a drunkard, to my knowledge, for I saw him so drunk that he could not conceal it to save his life. He was on the open streets of one of our county-seats, conspicuous to everybody. Besides this, he was pronounced a libertine. Of course these dark iniquities were not known when he began his brilliant career among us, preaching like peals of thunder amid the sheet-lighthing flashing all around; the people trembling, crying, crowding the altar, praying through, shouting the victory, and going away with brilliant faces and elastic tread, telling everybody to come to meeting and hear the greatest preacher that had trodden the globe since the days of John the Baptist and the Apostle Paul. They reported him as the most wonderfully Spirit-filled man they had ever seen. It was so, but it was the spirit of alcohol!

Eventually, amid the sweep of his victories, he inadvertently took too much, and it told its own story to the people, like a thunderbolt from a cloudless sky. They came to me weeping, crying out, "What shall I do? I got converted in Fairchild's meeting, but he is a fraud, a bad man. I suppose my religion is no account." I responded: "If Fairchild or Godbey converted you, it is no good; but if God converted you in Fairchild's meeting, it is just as good as if Paul had risen from his grave and preached every sermon, and as if Peter had leaped into life and conducted every altar service." Then they brightened up, and said, "Well, I know I did meet God. He forgave my sins and He gave me a new heart." I responded: "Then shout on, and pray for the preacher, that he may get religion too."

Many Holiness people think that God does not save souls through the instrumentality of unsaved people. Hear Jesus on the subject. The Sermon on the Mount, Matthew 7: "Not every one that saith unto me, Lord, Lord, shall enter into the kingdom of Heaven; but he that doeth the will of my Father which is in Heaven. Many will say to me in that day, Lord, Lord, we have prophesied (i. e., preached) in thy name, cast out devils (i. e., got people converted), and in thy name done many mighty works (i. e., had grand, sweeping revivals).'' But the Lord responds: ''I know ye not; depart into everlasting fire prepared for the devil and his angels.''

Mark this Judgment scene—preachers, in platoons, going away into everlasting punishment, while the people who were saved through their instrumentality go shouting up to Heaven.

John A. Murrill, the great Tennessee robber in pioneer days, was a powerful preacher, magnetizing the people by his intellectual brilliancy and his soul-enrapturing eloquence. He would preach his packed audience down on their knees crying for mercy; meanwhile his gang were stealing their horses. N. B. It is all plain if, in the light of God's truth, you will do your own thinking.

God alone can save, and He is no respecter of persons. He saves people through His truth. The Holy Spirit is everywhere ready to use His own truth in conviction, regeneration and sanctification. God will honor His own truth, even if preached by the devil. Thrilling scenes will move before the vision when the world stands before the great white throne; such as those preachers turned away and sinking in Hell, while the people to whom they preached go shouting up to Heaven.

Alexander the Great stands on the top-most round of fame's lofty ladder, as he conquered the whole world and wept because there was not another to conquer. When you go to Egypt, you will land at the great sea-port Alexandria, founded by him and named for him. You will, I trow, visit his tomb in the Prophet Daniel Mosque. He was first buried in Greece, in a golden coffin. It is very difficult to guard a gold coffin through the ages, as thieves will always be after it, so after while they took him out of it, putting him in a sarcophagus (stone coffin), and took him to Alexandria, Egypt.

He began his great work of conquering all the world at the early age of twenty, and finished it all in thirteen years; then he passed out of life, while yet in his youth, because, though he had conquered the whole world, he could not conquer his own depraved appetites, which so got the victory over him that he left the world in a disgraceful scene of debauchery. Of course grace was as free for him as for you and me, but God saves nobody without the co-operation of his own will.

(a) Oh, how wonderfully God used this brilliant young Greek! It is very doubtful whether there was another man in the world whom He could have used to execute the stupendous work which He wrought by this Macedonian juvenile. You think it strange that God would work great miracles through a man that knew Him not. God in Isaiah's prophecy, says: "Cyrus doeth my will, though he knoweth me not." He used Cyrus the Great to emancipate Israel out of Babylonian bondage; restoring them to their own land and rebuilding the temple and the walls of Jerusalem, actually taking money out of the royal treasury to do these great and mighty works.

From the beginning, Alexander knew that he was to conquer the world, though his nation was so small, comparatively but a handful, while the Persian empire reached her arms from the rising of the sun to the going down of the same. When Philip his father, vassal king of a small district, dying, left his throne to his son, he called up his army, and had the money-box capsized and the money counted. Finding but $35,-000, he divided it equally among his men, giving to each one his dollar, as he only had thirty-five thousand men in the army. They, with astonishment, said: "King, what have you left for yourself?" He answers, "My hopes." They say, "What are your hopes?" "Why! to conquer the whole world. I am not going to bother myself with the little sum of $35,000, so each one take your dollar and go ahead and do what you please with it."

It is wonderful how we have power to make others believe what we do, whether it is so or not so. Alexander just looked them in the face and talked to them so confidently as to superinduce their own belief in what he told them, and so he enthused them with the same glowing and transporting anticipation of possessing the whole world, with its time-honored kingdoms, gold and silver mines, and broad-spreading acres enveloping the entire globe. Alexander was so heroic, his men imbibing the same spirit, that nothing could stand against them.

Meanwhile Darius, the world's king, sitting on his throne in Persopolis, two thousand miles toward the rising sun; in the absence of the quick news which enlivens the present age (telegraphs and steam engines), and with so few people in the world who could read or write, the news traveling slowly, viva voce, and on a camel's back, when it did reach him, in such grandiloquent affirmations of their wonderful heroism and success, just soliloquized: "I will not trouble myself about that young fool; somebody will kill him in due time, and that will be the last of him." So he waits till not only months, but years, glide away; while meanwhile Alexander was moving hither and thither, with victory perching on the Grecian banner. Finally the king says: "I will have to settle that fellow," then he sends a great army to surround Alexander and his men, bag them, cut them into smithereens, and scatter their bones upon the face of the earth. They coil around him on the plains of Granicus, one hundred file deep, so that it will be impossible for a single one to escape. They close together and a terrible battle ensues, lasting a whole day and leaving forty thousand Persian soldiers dead on the field, while Alexander had not lost a man! Of course they had no fire-arms then, to kill people in sweeping avalanches of fire and brimstone, but they were armed with swords, spears and battle-axes. How strange that the Persians could not kill one of the Grecians!

You must not think that all the miracles that have transpired in this world are recorded in the Bible, which is simply our Savior's biography; the Old Testament excarnate, and the New incarnate. The contents of the Bible simply embrace the family of Jesus from Adam down to the manger of Bethlehem, so that we can all know that He is one of us, and hence competent to take our place under the violated law, redeeming us from sin, death and Hell. Read my books of travels, "Foot-prints of Jesus," "Around the World," and "Apocalyptic Angel"—and you will find many great miracles, wrought in different parts of the world and never mentioned in the Bible.

In this battle of Granicus, they all had equal chances, so far as arms were concerned. While these few Greeks slew the forty thousand Persians, how strange none of them got killed!

This battle paralyzed the world with astonishment, impressing the people that Alexander and his men were immortal gods in human form; so they let him alone quite awhile, years passing away. Meanwhile he was going from nation to nation carrying his conquests; then they saw that he was surely going to conquer the world if something could not be done. Consequenly, rendezvousing an overwhelming army, innumerable as the sands of the sea, they coiled around him on the fields of Issus. Then an awful battle ensued, winding up with one hundred thousand Persian soldiers dead on the field, deluging the plain with blood and heaping it with mountains of the slain, during those awful three days and nights of constant fighting. Meanwhile Alexander has no loss, but his men are scared exceedingly and deluged with the blood of the people they have killed.

The effect of this battle was felt in every nation under heaven, shaking and revolutionizing, and opening the eyes of the millions to see the trend of things— that the Greeks were actually going to conquer the whole world.

(b) The paralysis on the nations superinduced by the battle of Issus was so potently decisive in revolutionizing the popular mind, and in waking up the people to the momentous issues transpiring and impending, thus getting them ready for the stupendous ultimatum destined quickly to supervene, that, dazed, stupefied and appalled, they waited in unutter bewilderment for several years more. Then the Persian king makes a grand rally of all his subjects throughout the world, feeling that they certainly could down that paradoxical young Grecian. He so appeals to all the nobility and the princes of the earth that they see they are going to lose their offices, if something decisive is not done, for they all know that if Alexander succeeds, he will officer the whole world with Greeks. Therefore not only do they rendezvous an army from the plebeians (poor people), innumerable as the stars that glitter, but the patricians (nobility) turn out to a man, as it is conquer now or their offices will evanesce from them.

Again they coil their countless hosts around Alexander, on the fields of Arbela. A battle of a whole week ensues, winding up with the Greeks everywhere triumphant, and the royal army signally and utterly defeated. They can no longer hold their phalanx, but all military tactics are utterly given up, and they skedaddle in a promiscuous throng, no one thinking of anything but to escape for life. Meanwhile three hundred thousand are left dead on the field, among them just about all the nobility, so that there survived not a man influential enough to head another campaign. The government was gone, from the simple fact that the officers were dead. Darius himself, taking fright, fled from the field early in the conflict. He ran with all his might far away into India, the remotest country of the earth at that time, and Alexander on his track, overtaking him in the Deccan, i. e., the great southern peninsula of India running, down almost to the Equator.

When I preached in India, I was four times in Hyderabad, which Alexander founded during that visit; it now has, with its province, a population of eleven millions.

Alexander having pursued and overtaken Darius, the latter begins to sue for peace, observing: "Grecian, we have carried on this war long enough. I am in favor of peace. Rest assured I will treat you right; I will split the world in two in the middle and give you the choice half, and I will keep the other. So you and I will rule the world jointly." But Alexander responds, pointing up to the sun, then near the zenith (any one who has never been in India has no adequate conception of the solar brilliancy, power and glory): "Could this world have two suns? No, she could not, because they would burn her into a desert. Neither can it have two kings, so I will take it all. You are welcome to eat at my table as long as you live, if you will behave yourself; if not, you will wish you had."

I traveled six thousand miles and preached three months in India, night and day, without guide or interpreter. How do you explain it? Why, England has ruled that country for a hundred and fifty years. The normal effect of government is to impart the language of the rulers to their subjects; consequently, wherever I went through that vast country with its 300,000,000 inhabitants, when I spoke English the railroad officials everywhere understood me, as well as many others.

After his victory Alexander proceeded to take possession of the whole world, without a rival, as, in the great battle of Arbela, the ruling class were all slain, and none survived to make another fight. Of course Alexander puts the Greeks in every country under heaven, there being so few of them that they were just about all needed for rulers.

(c) Here you see clearly the reason why God gave Alexander the whole world. Oh, what a magnitudinous work He wrought through the instrumentality of that man whom He raised up to do that very work! And He would also gladly have saved his soul, if he had fully surrendered to and trusted Him.

While I preach the Bible Hell everywhere, and preach to Hell all who sin against light and knowledge, refusing to submit to God and believe His wonderful, saving truth, yet I only preach character to Hell and not individuals, as salvation is free for all and we know not how much light shines on any human soul While we know salvation is free for all, we know that all who walk in all the light they have—pagans, Mohammedans, Catholics (Greek and Roman), Protestants, Armenians, and all sorts of people in the world —receive the precious, cleansing blood.   (1 John 1: 7.) As John the Baptist says (John 1: 9), speaking of Jesus, "He is the true Light, which lighteth every man that cometh into the world." Do not conclude that there is no salvation but for those who historically know Christ. The Holy Spirit is the Spirit of Jesus (Acts 16: 6, 7), the executive of the Trinity, who alone can reveal Christ, and when the Son of God saves us, He does it through His omnipotent agent, the Holy Spirit, who is the Spirit of the Father (Acts 5: 3, 4). There are not three Gods—Father, Son and Holy Ghost—but only one, and three persons of that God.

In the great problem of salvation, every human spirit deals with God alone, who knows all about every one and makes no mistakes. All the people in the world who walk in all the light they have, get saved. "His mercy endureth for ever." Many people hold out till the very article of death, when they fully abandon all and cast themselves on the mercy of God in Christ, and get saved.

Of course we know not what God did for Alexander the Great in the article of death. All that we claim to know is that He did a great and mighty work through his instrumentality; in the dispensation of His merciful providence, raising him up, not to kill the millions of people, but to give the Gospel to the world. This God did through the Greek officers whom Alexander appointed over every nation under heaven, thus putting the Greek language in every home beneath the skies. When God needs a school, He raises it up, and utilizes it in a most marvelous way. The Greek government officers which Alexander placed over all the nations of the earth never dreamed of going to their places to teach the Greek language, yet that is precisely what they did.

The result was that, after three hundred years had rolled away (thus giving time for the people to get the language from their rulers), and the Son of God came on the earth, preaching His everlasting Gospel, Greek was actually the learned language of the world. Therefore when, pursuant to the Lord's commission (Matt. 28:19), the apostles divided the whole world out among themselves, each one going to his field of labor and preaching heroically till bloody martyrdom set him free, they all preached in the Greek language. So you see how wonderfully God provides!

When Alexander was pushing his conquests to the ends of the earth, and came to Jerusalem with his triumphant army, instead of their coming out to meet him in battle array, they all came out in religious procession, headed by the high priest in his royal robes and carrying the Bible (the portion of it they had in that day). The long procession of priests, Levites, prophets and scribes following on, the high priest opened to the prophecy of Daniel, and read to Alexander the words appertaining to himself and his great work, even using his name, i. e., Grecian. Alexander received it with the utmost appreciation, responding, "I knew it," i. e., the Spirit of the Lord had revealed to him a gleam of the great and mighty work he was to do on the earth.

(d) Paganism is very superstitious. With the mythologies of its poets, drawing on their imagination and giving the wonderful exploits of their gods, personifying them with human passions and investing them in the drapery of august divinities, the paganistic religion became so popular that it had no cross and waged no war against Adam the first. Rather, it honored him with the dignity of philosopher, orator, sculptor; invested him with sacerdotal robes, and even enthroned him in the temples of their gods, worshipping him as a god; as Paul tells us (1 Cor. 11), the heathens sacrificed to demons; aye, the excarnate demons which throng the air (Eph. 2:2), with Satan, their generalissimo, are actually worshipped by the heathen millions.

Paganism, with its demon worship, was the popular religion of the pre-Messianic ages, and we have the same now in the carnal churches, which allure the people with their popular religion. Take, for instance, a noted Delilah in one of our fashionable city churches. She was president of the Ladies' Aid Society, and a Sabbath-school teacher, and, during a revival, was personally leading the people forward to confess and to join the church; among others, her own beautiful daughter. To her she said: "Come along, my love; join the church and be a Christian. It shall not interfere with any of your pleasures; you shall go to all the balls." Of course the daughter went along, and was counted among the converts to Jesus, while her own proselytic mother had been used by Satan to make her own child "twofold more the child of Hell" than ever before (Matt. 23), her former sins being undisturbed, and the sin of hypocrisy in a religious profession being added to them, thus doubling the mess for the barbecues of Hell.

In those times the Jews were but a handful among the nations of the earth, isolated by their restrictive institutions until they wielded but very little influence among the nations. Hence the importance of the providential hands on the Gentile world. Oh, how wonderfully and paradoxically God dropped it down on the little Greek nation! Then, responsive to the magic spring, they rise among the nations of the earth like Mt. Hermon in Syria amid the vast catalogue of sacred mountains in the beautiful, historic Orient.

From the towers of Jerusalem and from many mountain peaks throughout Palestine, in our peregrinations, we enjoy a glorious view of Hermon, verifying the maxim often applied to the Apostle Peter and to the Methodist bishop, "primus inter pares" (first among his equals).

So God raised up the Greeks amid the hundreds of paganistic nations throughout the world, to give them the pure language in which He was going to send the message of salvation to every creature under the canopy of heaven.

(e) Pursuant to the providential call, while worshipping multitudes of mythical divinities, the creatures of their own poetic minds, the Greeks gladly obey. So, leaving all their comrades on the lower plain of illiteracy and superstition, they climb the heights of Parnassus, drink from the Pyerian fountain sparkling on its dizzy summit, and imbibe the true genius called poetry, oratory, philosophy, and the fine arts. They so magnetize the gaze of the whole world that, bewildered with the brilliancy of Greek originality, and dazed and electrified, they send their sons from other far-off lands to Athens and Corinth, to learn wisdom at the feet of the philosophers, poets and orators.

So the Greeks climb far above all their sister nations, abundantly thereby demonstrating the intervention of God's providence, in leading them to loftier heights, deeper depths and broader expanses of wisdom and intellectual culture; the grand culmination of the world's achievements in every ramification of human lore.

Supernally above all towers their language, which is itself a miracle in force, flexibility, music, elegance,

euphony, brevity, comprehensiveness and incorrupti-
bility; articulated with the human voice.

The English language is grand and glorious, and
eminently adapted to the colloquial and oratorical use
of the whole world. It is destined to become universal,
preparatory to the glorious millennial reign of Christ on
the earth; but it is not adapted to the revelation of
God's saving truth, because it is a mongrel. With
200,000 words, only 23,000 are original; the other
177,000 have been gathered from all the nations of
the earth. Therefore a revelation made in the English language would be subject to illimitable perver-
sions, misconstructions, and the most detrimental mis-
applications and misunderstandings.

But the Greek language, unlike the English, which
has no mechanism, is mechanical as a watch or a mus-
ical instrument, which must be put together just right,
or they will never keep time or make music. The
Greek language is not a Babel-gibberish, but a miracle
of the Lord, which He did not use His own people,
the Jews, to make, but this heathen nation; having the
glorious end in view of the evangelization of the
whole world.

Having used the Greeks to make the language, how
wonderfully God then used them to give it to all nations! He made them the rulers of the world, and at
the same time, though unconsciously, the teacher of
every nation under heaven; till His own Son came on
the earth, called His apostles, and commissioned them
to go into all the world and preach the Gospel to
every creature. At the same time, our blessed heavenly Father, in the long run of His providence through
the by-gone ages had been getting them all ready to

receive the message, of which their ancestors could not have understood a word; but the government officers having spoken and written Greek in their countries through the roll of several generations, they had actually learned the very language in which God has revealed His life-giving truth.

(f) Thus when, in God's time, His Son came on the earth, He fulfilled His own prophecies to send a "pure speech," i. e., one common language, understood by every nation under heaven) into the world, for, when Jesus and His apostles did all preach in Greek, it was understood by the heterogeneous nationalities of the globe.

It is thought by some that Matthew wrote his Gospel in the Hebrew, because he wrote it in Judea for the Jews, fifteen years after our Lord's ascension, but John Wesley, who was a profound scholar, shows up that he wrote it in Greek and that it was translated into Hebrew for the benefit of the Jews.

Follow Alexander through those thirteen years of constant victories, starting out with nothing and actually conquering the world, and you will see that God was with him as truly as He was with Moses when He used him to write the Pentateuch, giving His laws and institutions to Israel; or when he preached and worked miracles before Pharaoh of Egypt, thus miraculously leading Israel out of bondage, through the sea which He divided (permitting them to walk through on the dry ground), and leading them through the wilderness, by the cloud in the day and the pillar of fire by night. Or just as much as He was with Joshua when He helped him to gain the victory over the Amalekites, the Bashanites and the Heshbonites, and then arrested

Jordan's swelling flood and held it in check, accumulating like a mountain above them, till the Israelites all passed through into the Promised Land, where He wrought such stupendous miracles as knocking down the walls of Jericho. At Beth-horon Joshua even commanded the sun to stand still over Gibeon and the moon over the valley of Ajalon, and through the land of Canaan he was miraculously given the victory over seven nations greater than the Israelites. Thus seventeen years of triumphant conquest rolled away; then Joshua assembled Israel at Shiloh, and there gave them their inheritances in the land flowing with milk and honey and abounding in corn and wine.

Then, through the ages, God worked wonders through the most humble instrumentalities. For 450 years through the judges whom He raised up to deliver Israel, when, having sinned, they had again fallen into bondage. Last of all these judges, antecedently to the age of the kings, He gave them Samson, the greatest of the illustrious champions whose thrilling history crowns the heroic age of Israel. But they had so apostatized from God—the faithful dying and going to Heaven, and their sucessors, never having seen the mighty works of Jehovah, responsive to the depravity in all human hearts, falling away—that they refused Samson. Just as in all ages we see the churches drifting into darkness, becoming worldly, and falling into satanic bondage, oblivious of the brilliant testimonies of their fathers and mothers, who had been gloriously saved and beautifully sanctified, and who witnessed to these miracles of redeeming grace and dying love all their lives. But their children, never having received these glorious experiences, drift away, cap-

tured by Satan's lassoes which are always flying
through the air, adroitly wielded by his false prophets,
counterfeit professors, wizzards, witches and leger-
demainers scattered over the earth, who are always
spreading their nets to catch the unwary feet of the
improvident children, and to put the yoke of satanic
bondage on their necks, making them to serve the
brick-kilns and mortar-yards of Egyptian slavery.

Despite the mighty works which God had wrought
during the heroic age which followed Joshua and his
generation—by Othniel, the son-in-law of Caleb, Sham-
gar, and others—finally raising up Samson, the greatest of them all—they forsook Him. But He would
have delivered them from the bondage of the Philistines by Samson, if they had not been so blind that
they could not see the hand of God in the deliverer the
Lord had sent them. Under Samson's heroic leader-
ship, they might have conquered the world, because
you remember how, at Lehi, single-handed and alone,
with no weapon but the jaw-bone of a donkey, he slew
a thousand Philistines; heaping the bloody field with
mountains of the dead, notwithstanding they were
armed with swords, spears and battle-axes.

The great trouble was the fact that they had so
far apostatized from the God of Abraham, Isaac, Jacob,
Moses and Joshua that they could not see in Samson their own champion whom God had sent to deliver
them. Therefore they never utilized him at all, but
utterly ignored him, manifesting no appreciation of
God's miraculous intervention through his instrumentality, but, on the contrary, even betrayed him to his
enemies repeatedly. But he always conquered them,
even after this betrayal and capture, until he finally

fell under the seductive temptation of Delilah, who put him to sleep till she could clip his locks, the symbol of his Nazaritish vow and the presence of the Holy Ghost, through whom he had wrought all of his miracles.

In the old dispensation, the Nazarite, a total abstainer from wines and all sorts of intoxicants and narcotics, was God's sanctified man. As that was the symbolic dispensation, adumbrating the spiritual experience of the glorious Gospel age, in which you and I are permitted to live, the great lesson we learn from the Nazarite is that the secret of the power enjoyed by the truly sanctified consists in the fact that the Holy Ghost alone has His way with us, all rivals in the heart and life having been destroyed. Therefore we move amid constant victories over the world, the flesh, Satan, and all forms of temptation.

(g) It is thrilling and transporting to contemplate the manner in which God, in all ages, has had His hand on all nations, turning them as He turneth the rivers of water, and, unconsciously to them, fulfilling the prophecies through their instrumentality. Truth is the power God uses to save all the people in the world who will let Him save them. This truth is transmitted to the intellect and spirit through the medium of language, which is the vehicle of thought. All spoken languages are constantly undergoing changes, utterly imperceptible to the people who use them generation after generation. I have the English language in the New Testament, through the lapse of by-gone ages, from a barbaric dialect down to the present day. It exhibits so much change that you would find it very difficult to decipher and understand it, as in the version of Wicliffe, who translated in A. D. 1280; afterward Tyndale, and following him Cranmer; afterward the Geneva translation, and down to that of King James, which is the Bible common in all the Anglo-Saxon homes through the world to-day, having been translated under the supervision of that monarch three hundred years ago. When I was in London last April (1911), they celebrated the third centennial of the Authorized Version of the Bible.

Four times I have been in Greece, traveling around among the people and hearing their language as spoken at the present day. I find it so different from that of the New Testament (which I have been constantly using in Greek these fifty years; in the last thirty years using nothing else) that, when I speak to them they know nothing about it, and when they speak the current Greek to me, I cannot understand them.

You see here God's wonderful providence. When He had revealed His Word in the beautiful, classic Greek, then He took it out of all the mouths of living people, and let other languages come in and supply its place, because the normal effect of using a language is to corrupt it in many different ways—by ingress and agress; subtraction and addition; words becoming obsolete and dropping out, and others, emigrants from all other languages and dialects, coming in from multitudinous sources and finding a place in the vocabulary in current use. So when the Holy Ghost had inspired all the New Testament writers to reveal His wonderful truth to the world, then, in His providence, He proceeded to take the language out of the mouths of all nations, so that it might remain pure and uncontaminated by the provincialisms and slang phrases, which are always improvidently creeping into a spoken language. Therefore we have nothing to do but to go back to these dead languages (called "dead" because no living voices are now speaking them). Thus God, in His great and glorious merciful providence has preserved the fountain of His truth pure, uncontaminated, and we have nothing to do but to go thither and partake freely.

(h) Therefore in our Bible Schools we ought to have a Greek teacher in every one, so that the students can learn the pure and unadulterated Word, and use it in their evangelization of all nations. The most of the dangerous errors which are moving over the world like withering siroccoes and pestilential simooms have originated from errors in translation. That we may have the victory over all of these errors, and be able to dispense the pure truth to the world, we should take a short-cut in the matter, by learning the good old classic Greek, so that we can use it, carry it with us, and drink from the fountain of God's pure, limpid water, gurgling copiously from beneath His throne, and rolling on its limpid billows to satiate every thirsty soul in all the world

(i) The Old Testament is of infinite value, rich, sweet and precious, worth more than all the gold that ever glittered; infinitely valuable as an inspired history of our origin from the creative Hand, and of the wonderful plan of salvation which God miraculously launched through the instrumentality of His patriarchs and prophets, saints and heroes, from Abel down to Christ. The whole line of heroes was gloriously climaxed by God's own Son, the fulfilment of all the types, symbols and prophecies, they finding their final and glorious convergence, and eternal focalization in Him, the Prince of life and salvation, the Author of eternal redemption, and the glorious Victor of Mt. Calvary. Therefore we should diligently study the wonderful, inspired histories of the Old Testament.

It was written in Hebrew, therefore, if we have time, we should learn that beautiful original language. It is replete with light, life, beauty, grandeur and sublimity, leading us back to the days when God was alone in the vast universe, and commanded the elements so that the worlds, responsive to His mandate, rolled out from shapeless chaos, and obsequiously took their places in their appointed orbits in the void immense; moving out on their ceaseless peregrinatious around His effulgent throne, to wheel unshaken throughout the flight of endless ages.

(j) It is infinitely delightful and edifying to linger amid the glorious symbolism of Old Testament history, where we see the prophets called out by the great Jehovah and miraculously used by the Holy Ghost in preaching the great truths of the wonderful redemptive scheme. Meanwhile, God, in condescending mercy, corroborates all their wonderful utterances; whether revelatory of His dispensations of wisdom, grace, truth, righteousness and judgment; or denunciatory of the awful wickedness which has prevailed in the earth in all by-gone ages; or proclaiming the righteous retributions of the Almighty, vindicatory of His justice and proclamatory of His mercy, and at the same time electrifying the listening multitudes by the glorious hope which had spanned the world in rainbows of prophecy and promise ever since Jehovah

Himself preached the first Gospel sermon to the fallen twain, before their expulsion out of Eden. That sermon was: "The seed of the woman shall bruise the serpent's head," which was the Gospel in embryo; the nucleus of that wonderful truth which all the prophets, from Abel down, have proclaimed, enforced and magnified. Thus they concentrated the popular vision on the rising Star of Bethlehem, which flashed out on the Oriental sages, augmenting the holy constellations and leading them to the manger hallowed to contain the world's Messiah.

While we linger with delight and spell-bound edification and erudition amid the thrilling prophecies, glowing symbolisms and electrifying typology of the old dispensation, whose beauty, grandeur and sublimity eclipses all the poetry, oratory and transcendent philosophy of Hindu sages, Grecian heroes and Roman conquerors, we can do better than to abide amid these inspiring, edifying, transporting and electrifying symbols, types and shadows. It is our glorious privilege, not only to feast on these heavenly pabulations, but to move on to the wonderful Antitype, in whom all the shadows evanesce, absorbed by the glorious and eternal reality. All the prophecies culminate in the grand and glorious victory of their own fulfilment, and we are no longer left to study types, shadows and prophecies, but we hail the wonderful verifications of all these adumbrations, flashing out from the glorious Sun of Righteousness as He rises on the world, with healing in His wings, and gloriously culminating on the day of Pentecost, when He fulfilled the prophecies of John the Baptist, baptizing His disciples with the Holy Ghost and fire.

Pentecost is not a day, but a dispensation, which you and I are so fortunate as to enjoy. It is the noon-day of the glorious Sun of Righteousness, who declines not toward the horizon, but abides in the effulgent zenith of Pentecostal glory, flooding the celestial universe with the transcendent victories of entire sanctification, received and verified in the baptism of the Holy Ghost and fire, which He still pours on all fully abandoned, believing souls.

(k) Hence the glorious theme of Gospel preaching is not types, shadows and prophecies, which flood the Old Testament with victory and glory, so delectable to the Bible student, but we, who, in His good providence, are permitted to live in the Pentecostal dispensation, have all these types, shadows, symbols and adumbrations gloriously fulfilled in our wonderful Christ, "the Lamb of God that taketh away the sin of the world" (John 1:29). "We have this treasure in earthen vessels," and, in our investiture and endowment with this wonderful treasure, we are honored above all the kings, princes and potentates, Old Testament prophets and sages. This comes from the fact that we are freighted with the blessed historical Gospel, i. e., Christ mighty to save and strong to deliver; He having already conquered sin, death and Hell. Not only has He achieved the perfect victory on Calvary, but He even descended into Hell (1 Pet. 3:19), and there proclaimed His victory to the jubilant peers of the pandemonium, who had hounded Him from the manger to the cross. They plotted His death and thirsted for His blood, feeling assured that, if they could only kill Him, that settled the war of the ages, which they had been waging over this world, that they

might augment the restricted confines of the pandemonium, by the accession of this great world, over
which they had fought for four thousand years.
Therefore, when Jesus was arrested in Gethsemane
they began to shout the victory, and as news from the
bar of Annas, Caiaphas, Herod and Pilate reached
them in due order, giving new impetus to the sten-
torian shout, which finally received its sunburst when
the telephone of His death reached them, it evoked
such a roar as Hell never before had heard. "Victory! Victory has come at last!" And meanwhile a
thousand tall demons, on dusky pinion, are diligently
superscribing on the walls of the pandemonium that
electrifying proclamation—"Victory!"

In the middle of the superscription, a crash is
heard at the portals of the pandemonium, throwing the
gates wide open and concentrating the firey eyes of
all the demons thitherward. Behold! the Champion
of Mt. Calvary walks in, lightnings and rainbows flashing from His effulgent physiognomy. With the tread
of a conqueror, He walks round the walls of Hell, and
with His own hands pulls down the trophies of four
thousand years' successful warfare and treads them
beneath His triumphant feet. Finally, walking toward that old king, Diabolus, sitting on his ebon
throne in the center of the pandemonium, He drags
him down and puts His foot on his neck, thus verifying the first promise God made to fallen Adam and
Eve in Eden: "The seed of the woman shall bruise
the serpent's head." The light of His glory inter-
penetrates all the dark dungeons of the pandemonium.
The hierarchs of damnation all fall before Him, ac-
knowledging Him as conqueror.

(1) No wonder the glorified angels lean over the battlements of Heaven (1 Pet. 1:12), and linger, electrified, looking down on the Lord's heralds, standing on the streets of Cincinnati preaching to the dismal, Satan-ridden victims of slumdom the unsearchable riches of Christ. Gladly would they lay down their golden harps in place of silver trumpets, to blow all round this lost world to warn the wicked to flee from the wrath to come.

Up in Maine, amid the great pine forests, there lived an humble family. One afternoon the mother said to little John and Sallie: "Children, run away to neighbor Smith's" (only a mile along the beautiful path), to perform an errand. In that country snowstorms rise quickly. Though, when the mandate was given, the autumnal sky was serene and cloudless, and there was every prospect of a calm setting sun, yet soon Boreas arose with a tremendous roar and a lugubrious scowl. The winds evacuated their hiding-places, and dashed out for the delectable recreation of storm-races; speedily throwing their sable pinions athwart the firmament, and eclipsing the descending sun in sable night. They wrapped the great pine woods in sable clouds, and, dashing through them at race-horse speed, filled the elements with a loud roar of tall branches swept away and forests collapsing.

The family reached their pine-log cabin only to be appalled by the screams of the broken articulations of the mother, revealing the alarming absence of the little ones. Despite the howling storm, the falling snow and the clangor of the tree-tops, moving responsively to the roaring tempests, they, reckless of their own lives, rush out, and all that dismal, dreary night of winter, tempest and tornado, was heard, amid the clangor of the tree-tops and the thunder of the hurricane, in mournful, vociferous wails: ''Lost children! Lost children!''

The Lord has let me blow the silver trumpet for fifty-eight years. Of course my end is nigh, and this feeble body will soon peregrinate land and sea no more. My friends on all sides have begged me to quit preaching. As a rule, old preachers superannuate; not because they are a hundred years old, but because they have no calls. I have calls enough for a thousand men, clamorous on all sides for this precious treasure which we carry in these earthen vessels. Oh, that I had the wings of an angel and the trump of an archangel! Fein would I fly over land and sea to the ends of the earth, crying the alarm: ''Lost children! Lost children!''

You who read these pages, this moment hear the call of the juvenile Hebrew prophet, when he saw the temple filled with the glory of God and the seraphim hovering over it on radiant wings, shouting aloud: ''Who will go for us?'' He responds: ''Here am I; send me; send me. But what shall I do, for I am a man of unclean lips?'' ''Oh,'' they say, ''we are hunting for volunteers to press the Lord's war to the ends of the earth, and are so scarce of material that we cannot excuse anybody who has a willing heart. Unsanctified as you are, we take you now and put your name down on the army-roll of our heavenly King. He will attend to the qualification problem, as that belongs to His side, and all He wants on your part is perfect submission, doubtless faith and unfaltering obedience.'' Then an angel flies with a live coal from Heaven's altar, borne with the tongs (as God's fire is so holy that even an angel is unworthy to handle it), and puts it on the prophet's lips, and his sin is purged.

(m) "Sin" here is in the singular number because it means the evil personality, the sin-man, devil nature, transmitted to every human soul from Satan, through the fall. It can only be expurgated by the Blood; thus utterly eliminated away, burned up by the fires of the Holy Ghost, and utterly destroyed (Rom. 6:6).

The Bible is flooded with metaphors illustrating God's mighty works thus being felicitously accommodatory to our finite senses, so that we can receive, understand and appropriate them. Consequently we have innumerable allusions to the wonderful efficacy of the heavenly elixir of the cleansing Blood, and the consuming fires of the Holy Ghost.

Eph. 5:25: "Husbands, love your wives with divine love, as Christ loved the church, and gave Himself for her" (not it, as in the English version). As the church is the bride of Christ and the mother of God's children, therefore she cannot be represented by the neuter pronoun it, which stands for things without life, whereas the bride of Christ is filled with God's own life. "Purifying her by the washing of water through the Word, that He might present her to Himself a glorious church, having neither spot nor wrinkle nor any such thing." When Jesus baptized you with the Holy Ghost, giving you the blessed Holy Spirit as Sanctifier and Comforter (Acts 2:38), He (the Holy Spirit, the executive of the Trinity) applied the cleansing blood to the human spirit, expurgating all evil, eliminating depravity, purifying the heart, and removing all the wrinkles by His great, hot iron.

When He baptized me forty-three years ago, He ironed out many wrinkles, i. e., the Freemason, the Oddfellow, and all sorts of lodgery; the Methodist preacher; immersion and some other Baptist wrinkles, which I had along with not a few Methodist wrinkles; sectarianism and politics—all went to ashes in the consuming fires of the Holy Ghost.

The Blood is the omnipotent elixir which takes out all the spots, while the fire removes all the wrinkles, not only giving you a clean heart, but renewing a right spirit within you.

(n) Now, reader, history clearly shows up the fact that God, in His providence, wonderfully used Alexander the Great to give the whole world that beautiful Greek language, which He used the Greeks to make in order that He might give His precious, saving truth to all the world, which the wonderful mechanism, flexibility, euphony, force and felicity of diction of the Greek holds tight; despite all the studied schemes of false prophets, magicians and sophists to pervert and turn it to the destruction of the people. This wonderful language holds the truth tight in its iron grip forever, free for all to unlock the folding doors and receive a superabounding supply.

Yet we seriously fear that this man whom God used like Moses to do such a great work, giving the language to His own Son, and the apostles to the world—a benefaction so transcendent that it will take golden harps to proclaim it—yet we fear, and it is sad to think that this man, of so wonderful availability and so signally honored of God in the execution of this

stupendous and magnitudinous work in the interest
of His everlasting Gospel, lost his soul. N. B. ''Seek
ye first the kingdom of God and His righteousness, and
all these things will be added unto you'' (Matt. 6:33).

Yet the work of Alexander the Great was a wonderful blessing to millions in Heaven and others now
on the way, and it will so prove to the latest posterity.
God, in His perfect wisdom and lovingkindness, turns
everything into a blessing to His true people. (Rom.
8:28.) Pharaoh rejected the Gospel preached by
Moses, even though enforced by ten awful castigatory
judgments, sent him to humble his proud heart and
bring him to repentance. The waters turned to blood;
the frogs infesting the land and poisoning the atmosphere, so that the pestilence would have depopulated
the country if they had not been removed; the lice;
the flies; the murrain killing the animals; the hail
destroying the crops; the locusts eating up everything; the darkness filling the land; and the Destroying Angel making every home a morgue—all came
and went in vain, so far as Pharaoh's salvation was
concerned. Yet God made the Pharaohs a great blessing to His true people; raising them as the protectors
of the Holy Family, until they could multiply into in-
dependent nationality, thus becoming competent to
protect themselves.

Even the slavery was the very thing to most suc-
cessfully protect them from the perils of war which
then stalked like avenging specters throughout the
earth. Stronger nations would have annihilated the
Holy Family, if God had not protected them. He used
Egyptian slavery to do it, although when they became
competent to paddle their own canoe, He found it

necessary to utilize terrible castigatory judgments to secure their emancipation. N. B. Remember the words of Jesus (Matt. 6:33), and obey the same. Seek the kingdom of God first of all, resting assured that He will attend to everything else.

There is where the great mistake is made. Pharaoh was the first man to conquer the world and rule it. Though God wonderfully used him for great good in the protection of His people, giving them an asylum of security so they would not have to go to the battle-field, or do anything else to imperil their lives, and though He honored him with His two best preachers (Moses and Aaron), yet Pharaoh rejected all.

The master spirits of the world, who sought and accomplished great achievements, even the brilliant possession of the whole world, have made this sad mistake of not seeking the kingdom of God first of all. Oh, reader, let this not be your case, but settle the matter now, ringing out your life-long maxim: "Others may get saved and make Heaven their home, but I must, to an absolute certainty, with no defalcation about it!"

Heaven is free for all. You can get there if you will. Do not rest a day without experimental certainty in your own heart, witnessed to by the blessed Holy Spirit. Showers of blessings on you and your labors of love.

W. B. Godbey.

www.ingramcontent.com/pod-product-compliance
Lightning Source LLC
Chambersburg PA
CBHW030311030426
42337CB00012B/675